English Code 6

Grammar Book

Contents

Welcome!

1 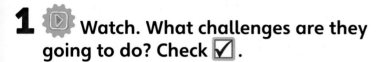 **Watch. What challenges are they going to do? Check** ✓ .

creating sentences ☐   looking for words ☐

singing songs ☐   solving puzzles ☐

working out codes ☐   writing poems ☐

2 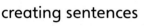 **Work in pairs. Watch and follow the instructions below.**

1 Note down the things Sophia can do. Compare with a partner.

2 What things can't Sophia do. Discuss.

3 Write down all the things you find out about Avatar. Compare with your partner.

4 What things would you like to find out about Avatar. Role-play asking and answering.

3 Read the presentation. Then write about someone else following the pattern.

CODE CRACKER

Meet my friend (Avatar). (Avatar) is from (outer space). <u>He's</u> from (outer space), but/and <u>he</u> loves (visiting planet Earth).

What is <u>he</u> like? <u>He</u> is (funny and friendly). Just like me! I'm (funny and friendly), too.

What does <u>he</u> look like? <u>He's</u> (tall and wearing white). I'm not (tall or wearing white). I'm (short and I'm wearing blue and green).

_____

_____

_____

_____

Language lab

LIKE

I will learn the different uses of **like**.

1 Read the dialog. What are Bella and Sam going to do after school? Underline.

Bella: Hello. You look lost.

Sam: Oh, hi. Yes, I'm new here. I'm looking for Classroom 5C.

Bella: That's my class, too! I'll walk you there.

Sam: Thanks! I'm Sam, by the way.

Bella: Nice to meet you. I'm Bella. So do you know anyone in our class?

Sam: No. But I have a cousin who's in 7th grade here. Her name's Kim Jones and she's 13.

Bella: I don't know her. What does she look like?

Sam: She's quite tall and she has long, brown hair.

Bella: OK. What is she like?

Sam: She's really funny. Sometimes she gets angry, but she forgets about it quickly. She likes basketball and skating.

Bella: What about you? What do you like?

Sam: I like math and chess.

Bella: Hey, me too! Let's play a game of chess after school today.

Sam: OK, great! Are we here?

Bella: Yes, this is 5C. Welcome!

Sam: Thanks, Bella.

🇬🇧 British	🇺🇸 American
Year 8	7th grade

2 Read again and match the questions to the answers.

1 Where is Bella taking Sam?

2 What does Kim look like?

3 What is Kim's personality like?

4 What does Kim like?

a She's tall with long, brown hair.

b basketball and skating

c to classroom 5C

d She's funny and she sometimes gets angry.

A question about personality: What **is** he **like**? He's shy, but friendly.

A question about appearance: What **does** he **look like**? He's short and thin.

A question about likes/dislikes: What **does** he **like**? He likes tennis and comic books.

3 Read the dialog again. Underline the questions with **like**.

4 Put the questions in order. Then read the online profiles and answer the questions.

1 Gill / What / look / does / like _____ ?
_____ .

2 is / like / she / What _____ ?
_____ .

3 does / What / like / she _____ ?
_____ .

4 does / like / What / look / Jake _____ ?
_____ .

5 is / like / What / he _____ ?
_____ .

6 he / What / like / does _____ ?
_____ .

 I'm Gill and I'm 13. I'm not very tall, but I'm good at volleyball. It's my favorite sport. My favorite subjects are history and science. My friends say I'm shy, but funny.

 My name's Jake and I'm 14. I'm quite tall and I have short hair. I like pop music and movies. My favorite movie is *Coco*. I'm a bit quiet, but friendly, too.

5 Make an online profile about an imaginary person.

6 Ask and answer about your profile in pairs.

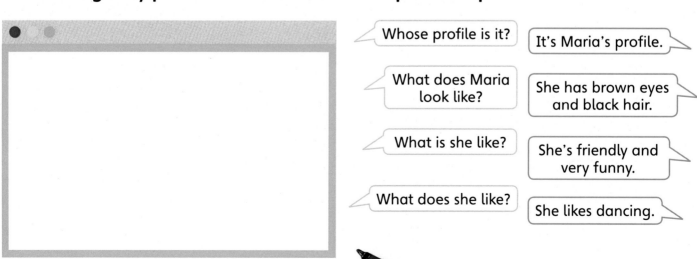

Whose profile is it?

It's Maria's profile.

What does Maria look like?

She has brown eyes and black hair.

What is she like?

She's friendly and very funny.

What does she like?

She likes dancing.

1 In the news

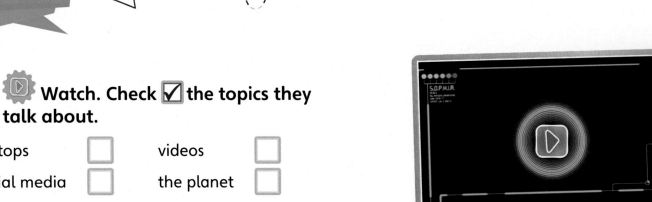

1 ▶️ **Watch. Check ☑ the topics they talk about.**

laptops ☐   videos ☐

social media ☐   the planet ☐

2 ▶️ **Read and complete the missing verbs. Watch to check.**

1   "This video _____ popular."

2   Zoe/Sasha said the video _____ popular.

3   "We _____ take care of the planet."

4   The blogger said we _____ take care of the planet.

5   "In my school we _____ about social media."

6   He said in his school they _____ about social media.

3 💬 **Write a sentence in the Simple Present about one of the topics. Then follow the pattern, saying your sentence for two partners to report.**

CODE CRACKER ⚙️

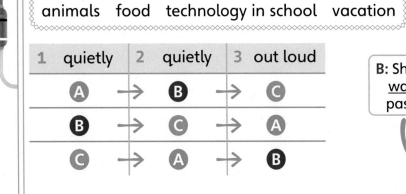

animals   food   technology in school   vacation

1 quietly	2 quietly	3 out loud
Ⓐ →	Ⓑ →	Ⓒ
Ⓑ →	Ⓒ →	Ⓐ
Ⓒ →	Ⓐ →	Ⓑ

_____

A: **I** want to have pasta for dinner.

B: She said that **she** wanted to have pasta for dinner.

C: You said that **you** wanted to have pasta for dinner.

Language lab 1
REPORTED SPEECH

I will learn to use reported speech.

1 Read the conversation. What's Tim going to do? Check ☑.

write for the class blog ☐   start a new blog ☐   make a vlog ☐

Tim: Hi, Vicky. Is your post for our class blog ready?

Vicky: No, sorry. I want to change the ending.

Tim: OK. So did you write about your trip to Kenya and the time you spent with the Maasai people?

Vicky: Yes, that's right. You said it was an interesting story.

Tim: Yes! Maria said that you had great photos with the Maasai children. Why don't you upload a few?

Vicky: I'm not sure. I'm worried about sharing photos online. I'll see if I have any good photos of the village or the giraffes.

Tim: OK, that would be great, too! You know, my dad booked a vacation in Italy and we're flying there in June. He said it was his dream to go to Rome.

Vicky: Why don't you make a vlog in Rome? You can share it on the blog.

Tim: That's a really good idea! I'm so excited about our trip!

2 What did Tim and Vicky say to each other? Choose the correct words.

1 Vicky said that his / her blog post was / wasn't ready.

2 She said that she wanted / didn't want to change the ending.

3 Tim said that Vicky's trip to Kenya was / wasn't an interesting story.

4 Tim said that he felt / didn't feel excited about their / our trip to Italy.

"I'm interested in **your** trip to Kenya, Vicky," said Tim.	He said that he was interested in **her** trip to Kenya.
"We are excited about **our** trip to Italy," said Tim.	He said that they were excited about **their** trip to Italy.
"I feel worried about uploading **my** photos," said Vicky.	She said that she felt worried about uploading **her** photos.

3 Read the conversation again. Underline sentences in reported speech.

4 Read and complete in reported speech.

be jump know live move not need

1 Vicky said that the Maasai _____ in small villages in Kenya.

2 She said that they _____ their houses from place to place.

3 A Maasai girl said to Vicky that she _____ a big house.

4 A Maasai boy said to Vicky that he _____ how to build a house.

5 Vicky said that the Maasai men _____ tall and _____ very high.

5 Write the sentences in 4 in direct speech.

1 "The Maasai _____."

2 "They _____."

3 "I _____."

4 "I _____."

5 "The Maasai men _____."

6 Complete the sentences about you using verbs in the Simple Present.

1 I live _____.

2 My friends _____.

3 My favorite _____.

4 People in my country _____.

5 Children my age _____.

7 💬 Work in groups. Take turns sharing your ideas from 6. Try to remember what your partners say.

8 💬 Write four things your partners said. Then check in your groups. Did you remember?

1 _____ said that _____ .

2 _____ said that _____ .

3 _____ said that _____ .

4 _____ said that _____ .

Tom said that he lived in the city center.

Yes, that's correct.

Language lab 2

REPORTED SPEECH QUESTIONS

I will learn about reporting an interview.

1 Read. How many questions does Sally report?

She reports _____ questions.

Hi, it's Sally here and this is our school vlog. Yesterday the famous author Peter Good visited us. He came to talk to us about his books and himself. He answered all of our questions and I'm here to report them.

Jack asked Peter how old he was. Peter said that he was 48.

Tom asked him if he had a pet and Peter said that he didn't.

Then it was Jenny's turn. She asked him if he wrote during the day or during the night. Peter said that he liked writing at night when his children were asleep.

I asked Peter what his favorite book character was. He said that he liked them all and didn't have a favorite one.

Lastly, our teacher asked Peter where he usually wrote his books. He said that he wrote in his garden and in cafés.

I hope you liked this week's vlog. Click again next week for a new story about our school! Bye for now!

| "Do you write every day?" | They asked him **if** he wrote every day. |
| "Where do you live?" | They asked **where** he lived. |

2 Rewrite the reported questions from 1 in direct speech.

1 "Mr. Good, _____ ?" asked Jack.

2 "_____ ?" asked Tom.

3 "_____ ?" asked Jenny.

4 "_____ ?" asked Sally.

5 "_____ ?" asked the teacher.

3 What other questions do you think the students asked Peter Good? Write two questions in reported speech.

1 They asked him _____ .

2 They asked him _____ .

2 Inspirational people

1 Watch. Check ☑ what each sentence is about.

Sentence 1

a race ☐   a trip ☐   a campaign ☐

Sentence 2

the ocean ☐   a desert ☐   space ☐

Sentence 3

games ☐   books ☐   computers ☐

2 Match to make sentences from 1. Watch to check.

1 She's the woman •   • who •   • books inspired thousands of children.

2 That was the day •   • whose •   • they first landed on the Moon.

3 He's an author •   • when •   • finished the marathon first.

3 Read. Find a pattern and complete the text with the phrases from the box.

CODE CRACKER

> Jane likes so much   Tom's mom owns (2)
> we bought chairs (2)   works at the furniture store (2)

He's the man who has that brown dog and who <u>lives on Green Street</u>.

He's the man who <u>lives on Green Street</u> and who 1 _____ .

He 2 _____ which 3 _____ .

4 _____ the furniture store where 5 _____ .

6 _____ which 7 _____ .

Language lab 1

RELATIVE CLAUSES

I will learn to use relative clauses.

1 Read the text. Why did Greta Thunberg become famous?

1 She changed the school system in Sweden. ☐

2 She was the first teenager to sail to New York from the UK. ☐

3 She made people her age start campaigning for the environment. ☐

Greta Thunberg

Greta Thunberg is an inspirational environmentalist from Sweden whose campaign "Fridays for Future" began in Stockholm in 2018 and then spread around the world. She was only 15 when she began to protest every Friday against climate change. Greta was determined to send out a strong message not just in Sweden, but across the world. And she did just that. Greta's campaign was the one that inspired teenagers from around the world to start a global movement for the environment. These are the young people who are known as "the Climate Kids." On August 14, 2019, Greta sailed from Plymouth, UK on a solar-powered boat and arrived 14 days later in New York, USA. That was the city where she gave her famous United Nations speech on September 23, 2019. In her speech, she said that adults should listen to children and save the Earth.

2 Read again. Match the sentences.

1 "Fridays for Future" was the campaign

2 Greta is the Swedish teenager

3 Plymouth was the city in the UK

4 It was in September 2019

5 Greta says it's children

a when she spoke in New York City.

b where Greta got on the solar-powered sailing boat.

c who adults should listen to.

d that started in 2018.

e whose campaign for the climate inspired many people.

3 Read again. Underline the relative clauses.

He's <u>the boy</u> **who / that** met Greta Thunberg.

She's <u>an environmentalist</u> **whose** speech at the UN made her famous.

It's <u>the campaign</u> **which / that** she started.

That's <u>the town</u> **where** she was born.

That was <u>the year</u> **when** she sailed across the Atlantic.

4 Read and match.

1	A place	•	• that	•	• you can buy books.	•	• a	sofa
2	A time	•	• whose	•	• takes care of animals.	•	• b	scientist
3	A person	•	• when	•	• job it is to work in a laboratory.	•	• c	bookstore
4	A thing	•	• where	•	• you can go on vacation.	•	• d	vet
5	A person	•	• who	•	• you can find in a furniture store.	•	• e	summer

5 Complete the rules with the correct words.

that (2)   when   where   which   who   whose

1   We use _____ or_____
   with things.

2   We use _____ with time.

3   We use _____ , _____ ,
   and _____ with people.

4   We use _____ with places.

6 Read and complete with relative pronouns.

1   They are my only friends _____ are determined to start a campaign.

2   There's the building _____ they are going to start a charity.

3   Saturday morning is the time _____ Edward writes his book.

4   Marie Skłodowska-Curie was a scientist _____ work changed the world.

5   Look! There's the book _____ you were looking for last week.

7 Choose two different ideas from the box and write definitions. Then work in pairs. Share your definitions and add more ideas.

bacteria   charity   doctor   lawyer   plastic
Saturday morning   the Earth   winter   your city

1   _____

   _____

2   _____

   _____

A doctor is someone who gives you medicine.

Yes. A doctor is someone who gives you medicine and who works at a hospital.

Language lab 2

USED TO

1 Look and read. Underline the things Grandma didn't have.

Maisy: Is this where you used to live?

Grandma: Yes, this was our cottage. We used to have problems with electricity, so my mom used to cook on a wood-burning stove. We also didn't have a regular bathtub or a shower in the bathroom!

Maisy: How did you get washed up then?

Grandma: We used to wash up in the sink.

Maisy: Where did you use to go shopping?

cottage

wood-burning stove

Grandma: Well, there weren't many stores. We used to get milk and eggs from the farm, and meat and vegetables from the local market.

Maisy: What about school?

Grandma: Our family didn't have a car, so I used to walk to school – it took an hour and a half. But I was determined to go to school. I wanted to study to become a nurse.

Maisy: And you did it! You're so brave and inspirational.

Grandma: Oh, thank you, Maisy.

sink

2 Read and circle.

1. Grandma used to (lives / live) in a cottage.
2. Her mother (doesn't / didn't) use to cook with electricity.
3. Her family didn't (use / used) to have a car.
4. Grandma (used / used to) walk to school.

> She **used to** eat a lot of fruit.
> We **didn't use to** travel much.
> **Did** they **use** to drink milk every day?
> Yes, they **did**. / No, they **didn't**.

3 What was your grandparents' childhood like? Write two sentences with used to and didn't use to. Compare your sentences in pairs.

1. In the past, children _____ .
2. They _____ .

4 Ask your partner about their life when they were 5 years old. Take turns.

Did you use to watch TV a lot when you were five?

No, I didn't. I used to play with my toys.

Let's earn money!

1 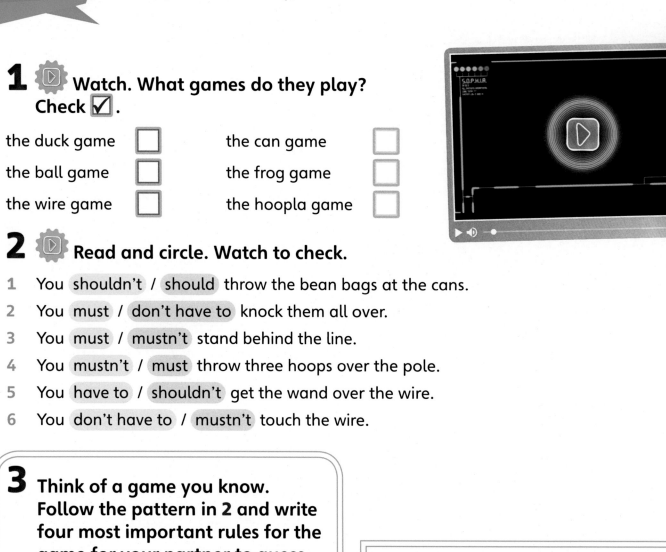 **Watch. What games do they play? Check ☑.**

the duck game ☐   the can game ☐

the ball game ☐   the frog game ☐

the wire game ☐   the hoopla game ☐

2 **Read and circle. Watch to check.**

1 You (shouldn't / should) throw the bean bags at the cans.

2 You (must / don't have to) knock them all over.

3 You (must / mustn't) stand behind the line.

4 You (mustn't / must) throw three hoops over the pole.

5 You (have to / shouldn't) get the wand over the wire.

6 You (don't have to / mustn't) touch the wire.

3 **Think of a game you know. Follow the pattern in 2 and write four most important rules for the game for your partner to guess its name.**

CODE CRACKER

Game: _____

1 _____

2 _____

3 _____

4 _____

Language lab 1

OBLIGATION AND ADVICE

> I will learn how to talk about obligation and advice.

1 Read. Label the photos with *Sarah* or *Lucy*.

Lucy:

I'd like to buy a new bike. To save money for it, I can sell things I knit. My grandma taught me how to make scarves, socks, and hats. I should write an advertisement about my knitting on my social media. I don't have to upload photos, but it's a good idea to show what I can make. The only thing is that I'll need time to do the knitting and I must buy good wool. I have to think about all this when I decide on a price for each thing.

Sarah:

I need to save money for my school trip to Canada in September, so I'm going to work this summer. I'm going to walk my neighbors' dogs every day. I have to walk four dogs twice a day, so it's a good idea to exercise a bit before I start work. I must be careful when I cross the road and I mustn't let the dogs get too dirty. My brother says I should get new sneakers, but I don't have to. I have an old pair that's really comfortable.

_____

_____

2 Read again. Write *Yes* or *No*.

1   Lucy doesn't have to write an advertisement but it's a good idea.   _____

2   Lucy shouldn't upload photos of scarves, socks, and hats.   _____

3   Sarah has to be fit to walk four dogs twice a day.   _____

4   Sarah must stop the dogs from getting dirty.   _____

3 Read again. Underline should, must, mustn't, have to, and don't have to **together with the verbs that follow them.**

Advice	Obligation
You **should** sell your scarves on the internet.	I **have to** carry water for the dogs.
	I **must work** hard to earn money.
You **shouldn't** sell them too expensive.	I **mustn't forget** to include prices in the advertisement.
	No obligation
	I **don't have to** walk them very early in the morning.

4 Choose the correct words.

1 Mark draws great pictures! He (should / shouldn't) sell them at the School Fair.

2 We (shouldn't / must) buy products that are made of plastic. It's bad for the environment.

3 You (have to / don't have to) buy things at the School Fair. Only if you want to.

4 Gill (doesn't have to / must) start saving if she wants to go on the school trip. There's not much time left.

5 For the science project, students (have to / should) invent a new way to recycle plastic.

5 Complete the dialog. Use the words in the box.

> don't have to   have to (5)   mustn't (2)   should (2)

Lia: Hey, Carl. What's that?

Carl: It's a new game I've programmed.

Lia: Can I play it?

Carl: I'm still working on it. And I
1 _____ finish it before
Friday for the School Fair.

Lia: So what do you 2 _____
do in this game?

Carl: You 3 _____ hit the
blue balls to get points, but you
4 _____ hit the white
squares or the green triangles. You
5 _____ remember this
if you want to score a lot of points.

Lia: OK. It looks easy, and fun! I think you
6 _____ sell it.

Carl: That's the idea. It'll be 50 cents to
download the app. I'll use the money
to take a programming class.

Lia: I'll download it! But I
7 _____ ask my
dad first because he says I
8 _____ download
anything without asking.

Carl: Yeah, he's right. You
9 _____ pay. I'll
send you a code to download it
for free. Now, sorry, Lia. But I really
10 _____ work on this.
See you later.

6 ⚙️ 💬 Work in pairs.

1 Create a new game that you would like to play on your smartphone, tablet, or computer.

2 Talk about what you have to do and what you mustn't do in the game.

3 Change partners. Present your game to your new partner.

4 Ask questions to find out more about your partner's game.

This new game is called …

What do you have to do in it?

You have to …
You mustn't …

Language lab 2

REQUESTS FOR HELP

I will ask and respond to requests for help.

1 Read. Underline three requests.

Hi Ally,

How's it going? Have you finished editing the photos from the School Fair? Would you do me a favor and send me three photos, please? I'm writing about the fair for our class blog and I want to include them in my post. Could you email them to me today? Also, how many T-shirts did Ed and Mike sell at the fair? Do you know?

Thanks,

Mina

Hey Mina,

Yes, the photos are ready. I'm attaching five for you to choose. The School Fair went really well. Ed and Mike sold 20 T-shirts, so they made $160! And I made $40 with the face painting. Isn't that great? We almost have the money we need for our class library. Could you tell me when your post is up? I'd like to read it.

Bye for now,

Ally

2 Read the answers and write polite requests. Use **could** or **would** and the words in parentheses.

> **Would / Could you** (do me a favor and) open the window, please?
>
> **Could I / we** use your book, please?

1 A: _____ ? (borrow)

   B: Sure. My phone is on the table.

2 A: _____ ? (a favor)

   B: I can take a photo of you. No problem.

3 A: _____ ? (the time)

   B: It's three o'clock.

4 A: _____ ? (play with you)

   B: Of course. Let's start a new game.

3 Write two requests. Then work in pairs. Practice asking and responding to each other's requests.

Could we borrow your ball, please?

Sure, you can play with it.

1 _____

2 _____

Food for the future!

1 ▶ **Watch. Check ☑ the nouns you can hear.**

basket ☐   cake ☐   dairy ☐

diet ☐   food ☐   insects ☐

rooftops ☐   sugar ☐   teeth ☐

2 ▶ **Complete with the words from the box. Then circle PR (prediction), I (intention), or PL (plan). Watch to check.**

> be going to   eat (2)   grow   will (2)

1   In the future food _____ _____ on rooftops.   PR   I   PL

2   My teeth hurt. I _____ _____ less sugar.   PR   I   PL

3   In 2030 I think everyone _____ _____ insects.   PR   I   PL

3 **Read the sentences and look at the labels. Check ☑ the correct labels. Correct the wrong ones.**

CODE CRACKER

1   I'm going to stop having pasta for dinner every day.
   Intention ☐
   _____

2   I think we'll eat less meat in the future.
   Plan ☐
   _____

3   There isn't any olive oil. I'll use sunflower oil instead.
   Decision in the moment ☐
   _____

4   They're having lunch at that vegan restaurant tomorrow.
   Prediction ☐
   _____

5   Peter's going to try to eat more fiber and protein.
   Decision in the moment ☐
   _____

Language lab 1

TALKING ABOUT THE FUTURE

I will learn how to talk about the future.

1 Read. What change has Fred decided to make? Check ☑.

1   eat more apples ☐   2   learn to cook better ☐   3   eat less sugar ☐

Fred: Tomorrow we're visiting a farm, Grandpa. It's called the Halton Farm and they grow apples there.

Grandpa: Oh, that's a nice farm. It's going to be sunny tomorrow, so I'm sure you'll have a great time. Are you going to help pick the apples?

Fred: I think so, yes. I'll send a text to my friend Emily and ask her. She knows more about the trip because she helped Mrs. Elliot organize it.

Grandpa: Well, take a bag with you just in case. They grow a lot of different types of apple at Halton Farm. My favorite apples are the Fuji and the Cortland apples.

Fred: I don't know much about apples, Grandpa. I'm sure I'll learn more tomorrow.

Grandpa: You will! Bring some apples home and we can make your favorite apple pie.

Fred: Yum! OK, but I told you – I'm going to eat less sugary food from now on.

Grandpa: I know, I know. We'll use less sugar in the apple pie.

2 Read again. Choose the correct words.

1   Fred is / isn't visiting a farm tomorrow.

2   It is / isn't going to be a nice day to spend at the farm.

3   Grandpa thinks Fred will / won't enjoy the visit.

4   Fred will ask / tell Emily about picking apples.

5   Fred knows / doesn't know a lot about the different types of apples.

6   Fred is / isn't going to change his diet.

> I think it**'ll rain** this week. (prediction)
>
> We**'ll make** a pie with these apples. (decision in the moment)
>
> It**'s going to be** a great school trip. (prediction)
>
> We**'re going to think** more about the food we eat. (intention)
>
> I**'m walking** to the farmer's market tomorrow morning. (plan)

3 Read again. Underline the following:

- predictions and decisions made in the moment with *will* in blue
- predictions and intentions with *be going* to in green
- definite plans with Present Progressive in black

4 Circle the correct words.

When I grow up I 1 **will be** / **'m going to be** a food taster – that's a person who gets paid to try food. I want to be an ice cream taster. Yes, this job exists and it 2 **'s going to be** / **is being** great! An ice cream taster starts work early and he or she spends about five hours tasting different flavors of ice cream. Also, I 3 **'m trying** / **'m going to try** to create new flavors. I think I 4 **'m starting** / **'ll start** experimenting this evening. Mom 5 **will stop** / **is stopping** at the store on her way back from work, so I 6 **'m asking** / **'ll ask** her to bring home a lot of ice cream.

5 Reorder the questions.

1 are   tonight?   having   What   you   for   dinner

_____

2 will   grow   How   food   we   100   years?   in

_____

3 are   cook   going   you   to   for   something   me?   When

_____

4 Is   to   next   change   going   in   20   the   years?   food

_____

6 Write your answers to the questions in 5. Then take turns asking and answering with a partner.

1 _____

2 _____

3 _____

4 _____

7 What food will people eat 100 years from now? Create a list of dishes for a typical day in the future and draw pictures. Then explain your predictions in small groups.

Language lab 2

MIGHT AND WILL

> I will talk about future possibilities.

1 Read and circle.

Martha / Rob thinks our diet won't change a lot in the near future.

How will our diet change in the near future?

People's diet will continue to change. I'm sure more people will eat less meat. I also know a lot of vegans, who don't eat any meat or animal products like eggs and milk. Some of my friends might become vegan, too, or vegetarian. I won't become a vegan because I like dairy products too much! In the future, I think people will have healthier diets because there's a lot more information about food.

Martha, 12 years old

I don't think what we eat will change. We will always need fruit, vegetables, meat, fish, and dairy products. And we'll always have breakfast, lunch, and dinner. We might use new technology to cook food faster and in a healthier way – I'm not sure. Also, the food might taste better if it's cooked differently. Or maybe it'll taste worse. Who knows?

Rob, 13 years old

2 Read and circle T (True) or F (False).

Martha thinks …

1   people's diet won't stay the same in the near future.   T / F

2   there will soon be more vegans than vegetarians.   T / F

3   she might become vegan in the near future.   T / F

Rob thinks …

4   the way we cook will definitely change.   T / F

5   it's possible we'll eat tastier food in the future.   T / F

> It **will be** cheaper to buy organic food. I'm sure.
>
> **There might not be** any small farms left. It's possible.

3 Complete the ideas with will, won't, might, or might not. Compare your ideas with a partner. Give reasons for your ideas.

In the near future …

1   we _____ grow different kinds of food.

2   many people _____ eat meat.

3   people _____ prepare more meals.

4   intensive farming _____ stop.

5 The ancient world

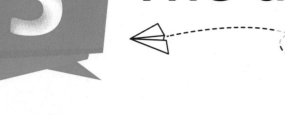

1 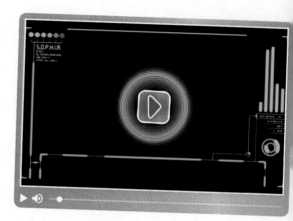 Watch. What do they talk about?
Check ☑ or cross ☒.

 1
 2
 3
 4

2 Complete with the verbs in the Passive. Watch to check.

1 The pyramids _____ with limestone.

2 The mummies _____ with their treasure.

3 Hieroglyphics _____ for writing.

build
bury
use

3 Read. What's wrong? Rewrite the sentences with incorrect information and check ☑ the correct ones.

CODE CRACKER

1 Papyrus was used by the Chinese. ☐

_____

2 Plastic was made with leaves of the papyrus plant. ☐

_____

3 The coffin of King Tut was found by Howard Carter, an archeologist. ☐

_____

4 King Tut's mummy was buried with amazing treasure. ☐

_____

5 The Great Pyramid in London was built by over 20,000 people. ☐

_____

Language lab 1

PAST PASSIVE

1 Read the fact files. Which building is older? Check ☑.

the Parthenon ☐   the Colosseum ☐

The ancient Egyptian civilization was one of the most important civilizations of the ancient world. The ancient Greek and ancient Roman civilizations were also as important. Here are two monuments from those civilizations.

The Parthenon

This famous temple is located in Athens, Greece. It was built between 447 BCE and 432 BCE when Pericles ruled the city. The Parthenon was made using limestone and 22,000 tons of marble, a type of hard stone. That's a lot of marble! It was designed by Phidias, who was a famous artist, and by the architects Ictinus and Callicrates.

The Colosseum

The Colosseum was a very famous theater in ancient Rome, which was used for gladiators' battles and other events. It had four floors and 50,000 people could sit in it and watch. Emperor Vespasian began to build it in 72 CE and it was completed in 80 CE by his son Titus. It is still visited today, although parts of it were destroyed.

2 Read and circle the correct answer.

1   The Parthenon and the Colosseum (were / weren't) built a few years ago.

2   Athens (was / wasn't) ruled by Pericles in 447 BCE.

3   Gladiators' battles (were / weren't) fought in the Colosseum.

4   The Parthenon (was / wasn't) designed by one architect.

5   The Colosseum (was / wasn't) completed by Emperor Vespasian's son.

3 Read again. Underline verbs in the Past Passive.

Active

They **completed** the Parthenon in 432 BCE.

Phidias **designed** it.

They **used** both buildings for different events.

Passive

The Parthenon **was completed** in 432 BCE.

It **was designed** by Phidias.

Both buildings **were used** for different events.

4 Rewrite the sentences in the Passive. When necessary use by to say who did the action.

1 The ancient Greeks didn't invent ink. The ancient Egyptians and Chinese invented it.

Ink wasn't _____

_____

_____ .

2 They didn't build the Giza Pyramids with marble. They built them with limestone.

The Giza Pyramids _____

_____

_____ .

3 Archaeologists discovered hundreds of Moai statues on Easter Island.

_____

_____ .

4 People played backgammon in Persia around 3,000 BCE.

_____

_____ .

5 Complete the text with the Past Active or Passive of the verbs in parentheses.

The buried army

Chinese farmers near the city of Xi'an 1 ___discovered___ (discover) the Terracotta Army in 1974. They were digging to find water when a big soldier figure 2 _____ (find) in the ground. More than a thousand life-size soldiers and horses 3 _____ (bury) in the area. The soldiers 4 _____ (protect) the tomb of Qin Shi Huangdi, the first emperor of China, and all the figures of soldiers and horses 5 _____ (make) of terracotta clay. Each soldier 6 _____ (look) different and was more than 2 meters tall! It was an amazing discovery!

6 Find out about ancient inventions and archaeological discoveries. Use the verbs to write sentences in the Past Passive. Then check if your partner knows about them.

build   design   discover   find   make

_____was/were built_____

_____

_____

_____

_____

The pyramid of Chichén Itzá was built in …

… in Mexico. It was built in Mexico.

Correct!

Language lab 2

PAST PASSIVE QUESTIONS

I will talk about the history of a place.

1 Read. Where is the building in the photo? Underline the country.

Paul: Wow! That looks amazing. Who took that photo?

Fatima: My friend Amy took it in Petra. She went there on vacation.

Paul: Cool. So when was this built?

Fatima: Let me check. The search engine says it was probably built around 312 BCE. It's really old!

Paul: Wasn't Petra voted one of the New Seven Wonders of the World?

Fatima: Yes, it was. There are lots of buildings made in stone. Amy took a photo of this one, called "The Treasury."

Paul: So when was Petra discovered?

Fatima: Well, it says here that up to 30,000 people used to live there, but then the city was abandoned. It was discovered again in 1812.

Paul: Cool. I'd love to go there one day. Petra's in Egypt, isn't it?

Fatima: In Jordan! I thought you were good at geography!

The Treasury in Petra

2 Read again. Complete the questions and match them to the answers.

> Was   When was   Who was

1 _____ the photo taken by?

2 _____ Petra built?

3 _____ Petra voted one of the New Seven Wonders of the World?

a Yes, it was.

b Around 312 BCE.

c Fatima's friend, Amy.

3 Order the words to write questions.

1 Parthenon / the / When / completed / was

_____ ?

2 the / Where / built / was / Colosseum

_____ ?

3 was / near Xi'an / found / What

_____ ?

> **Was** Petra **discovered** in 1812? Yes, it **was.** / No, it **wasn't.**
>
> **Were** any statues **found** there? Yes, there **were.** / No, there **weren't.**

4 Answer the questions in 3. Work in pairs and test each other.

25

On the move!

1 ▶ **Watch. How many sentences do the players get right in time? Check ✓.**

one sentence ☐   two sentences ☐

three sentence ☐   zero sentences ☐

2 ▶ **Read and complete with a verb in the correct form. Watch to check.**

1   I've been _____ a lot of places.

2   I have _____ meeting a lot of people.

3   I have _____ _____ about transportation.

4   I've just been _____ and bought a lot of presents.

🇬🇧	British
	transport
🇺🇸	American
	transportation

3 **Look at the dialog. Think of another destination and rewrite the dialog for it. Follow the pattern.**

CODE CRACKER ⚙️⚙️⚙️

A: I'm in <u>London</u>! I've been <u>going to museums</u>.

B: Oh really? <u>What kind of museums</u>?

A: <u>History and science museums.</u>

B: What did you <u>see in the history museum</u>?

A: <u>I saw statues and coins.</u>

Destination _____

A: _____

B: _____

A: _____

B: _____

A: _____

Language lab 1

PRESENT PERFECT PROGRESSIVE

I will learn about the Present Perfect Progressive.

1 Read the interview. What countries has Mason visited?

Mason's visited _____ .

Do you think you could travel around the world in 80 days?

We talk to Mason Moore, who has been traveling around the world without taking a single flight!

Where are you now?

I'm near Japan. I've been sailing all night on a ship from South Korea.

How long have you been traveling?

I've been traveling for 56 days – nearly two months!

What vehicles have you used?

Almost all of them! The only transportation that I haven't used is an airplane. I've been sailing, and riding trains, trams, scooters, and even camels.

What problems have you had so far?

I had a lot of delays on trains through Greece. I missed a bus in Egypt. Oh, and sickness. I've been having stomach problems and I haven't been sleeping very well lately. But it's still been amazing.

Are you looking forward to going back home?

Well, I really miss my friends and family. But I've decided to move to China for a year or maybe longer. I'd like to learn Mandarin and work here.

2 Read again. Circle T (True) or F (False).

1 Mason has been traveling around the world.   T / F

2 He has been driving from South Korea to Japan.   T / F

3 He hasn't been sleeping well on his journey.   T / F

4 He has been traveling for three months.   T / F

I've **been sailing** in this boat since eight o'clock this morning.

We **haven't been living** in Greece for long.

How long **has she been waiting** for the bus? She's **been waiting** for an hour.

Have they been traveling for long? Yes, they **have**. / No, they **haven't**.

3 Read again. Underline the sentences with Present Perfect Progressive.

Remember!

for = a duration of time

since = from a past date

4 Complete the sentences. Circle for or since.

1 My uncle has been working in China for / since 2018.

2 They've been sleeping for / since 6 o'clock. They must be tired.

3 I've been studying history for / since an hour. Can I take a break?

4 Ellie and her sister have been traveling around Europe for / since three months. They love it!

5 You've been living in this apartment for / since May. Do you like it?

5 Complete the sentences. Use the Present Perfect Progressive.

1 I _____ (read) the book you gave me. I have 20 more pages left.

2 A: _____ you_____ (practice) French with Pierre?

   B: Yes, we _____ (speak) French for two hours today.

3 My brother is on an exchange program in Spain. He _____ (not travel) much because he has to go to class.

4 How long _____ they _____ (learn) English? They speak really well.

5 Sarah _____ (dream) of traveling to Japan for years and years. Now her dream is going to come true.

6 Think of four questions to ask your partner. Use the Present Perfect Progressive.

1 How long _____ ?

2 What _____ ?

3 Where _____ ?

4 Have you _____ ?

7 Ask and answer your questions from 6. Use since and for in your answers. Ask an extra question to find out more.

How long have you been playing the piano?

I've been playing the piano since I was eight years old.

And do you enjoy it?

Yes, I really like it!

Language lab 2

JUST, ALREADY, YET, STILL

I will talk about recent events.

1 Read. Where are Sally and Lisa now? Underline.

My friend Lisa and I are going to travel for a year before starting college. We're leaving in a week, but we've already decided which countries to visit. Follow us around the world!

March 10

We've been in Istanbul, Turkey since Monday. We've already seen so many things! This is a view of Hagia Sophia. We haven't been to the Topkapi Palace Museum yet. We're going tomorrow. We want to see its great jewel collection.

March 21

We've just arrived in our hotel in Bali! We still haven't swum, but the sea looks amazing. I can't wait to dive in! We're going to watch the Kecak fire dance tonight. The Balinese have performed this dance for over 80 years.

April 3

Is this China? No! We're in Chinatown, in San Francisco. We arrived in the United States two hours ago. We haven't had time to walk around the city yet.

2 Circle the correct words.

Hi, Mom! We're on our way home. I've
1 still / yet / **just** gone through security. Lisa
2 still / **yet** / already hasn't finished with the passport control. While I'm waiting, I'll have a look at the stores. I've 3 **already** / yet / still bought you a present, but I haven't got Mike anything 4 just / **yet** / already . Do you think he'd like a T-shirt from Chile?

She's **just** booked a hotel.

They've **already** seen the museum.

Has the plane taken off **yet**?

No, they **still** haven't finished check-in.

🇬🇧 British	🇺🇸 American
university	college

3 Think and write about one thing you have already done and one thing you haven't done yet. Tell a partner.

I've already traveled by plane.

I haven't visited China yet.

1 _____ .

2 _____ .

7 I hate it when ...

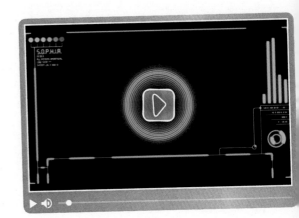

1 Watch. How many answers do they get right and wrong? Write a number.

a ✓ _____   b ✗ _____

2 Complete with the verbs in the correct form. Then match the questions to the answers. Watch to check.

> be   hold   see

1 _____ you ever _____ skiing?   a   Yes, it felt soft and had a long body.

2 _____ you ever _____ a shark?   b   Yes, I went last winter and fell over all the time.

3 _____ you ever _____ a snake?   c   Yes, I saw one in the ocean last summer.

3 Read the questions and guess the category for each set. Then choose a question from each category and answer it for you.

CODE CRACKER

1 _____

Have you ever traveled by train?

Have you ever seen an ancient monument?

2 _____

Have you ever scored a goal?

Have you ever run a race?

3 _____

Have you ever made a cake?

Have you ever eaten octopus?

1 _____

2 _____

3 _____

Language lab 1

PRESENT PERFECT AND SIMPLE PAST

I will learn about the Present Perfect and Simple Past.

1 Read. Who has done more things mentioned in the article? Check ☑.

 Andy ☐

 Lucy ☐

Andy: Lucy, I'm reading an article called "Things you must do before you're 25." Have you seen it?

Lucy: Yes, I have. And I've already done most things on the list!

Andy: Me too. Look. I've swum in a waterfall. I did that last year in Spain.

Lucy: OK. I haven't done that. But I've looked down from the top of a skyscraper. I did that last month in New York City.

Andy: Cool! Did you go to the Empire State Building?

Lucy: That's right. Have you ever been to the Grand Canyon?

Andy: Erm … no, I haven't.

Lucy: Me neither.

Andy: Have you ever walked on the Great Wall of China? I did that when I was eight years old.

Lucy: Well, no, I haven't done that. Have you ever snorkeled in a coral reef?

Andy: Sure, I've done that in Egypt, in the Red Sea. I also rode a camel when I was there last winter.

Lucy: I've ridden a camel, too! But not in Egypt. I rode one in Morocco two years ago!

Mario: Please be quiet, you two. And stop showing off!

2 Read again. Circle T (True) or F (False).

1 Lucy has read the article Andy is reading. T / F
2 Lucy didn't swim in a waterfall last year. T / F
3 Andy and Lucy have been to the Grand Canyon. T / F
4 Andy hasn't snorkeled in the Red Sea. T / F
5 Lucy has ridden a camel in Egypt. T / F

3 Read again. Underline the verbs in the Present Perfect and circle the verbs in the Simple Past.

> **Have** you **ever ridden** a camel?
>
> Yes, I **have**.
>
> When **did** you **do** that?
>
> I **rode** a camel in Morocco two years ago.

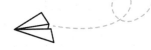

4 Circle the correct words.

1 Ben (has never missed / never missed) the start of class. He's always on time.

2 I (went / have been) to the top floor in the afternoon, but I (didn't look / haven't looked) down. Scary!

3 **A:** (Did you text / Have you texted) Mary yesterday?

  B: No, because I (dropped / have dropped) my phone after school and it's not working now.

4 **A:** (Did they ever travel / Have they ever traveled) in Europe?

  B: Yes, they (drove / have driven) around France and Italy last summer.

5 Complete the text with the Present Perfect or the Simple Past form of the verbs.

We **1** _____ (leave) Turkey six weeks ago for the student exchange. We talk to our families over the internet every day, so we **2** _____ (not turn) it off at all.

Yesterday, I **3** _____ (oversleep), so I missed the trip to the Statue of Liberty. In the afternoon, we **4** _____ (go) to Yankee Stadium. I love baseball! Tomorrow morning, we're going to go to the Empire State Building. I **5** _____ (not go) up a skyscraper yet, so I'm really excited. In the afternoon, we're going to watch the movie *King Kong*. I **6** _____ (already, see) it, so I'm going to go shopping instead.

6 Ask a partner if these things have ever happened to him/her. If yes, find out more details.

buy something and then find it cheaper somewhere else

cook something horrible

forget someone's name

take someone else's backpack by mistake

watch a scary movie alone

Have you ever cooked something horrible?

Yes, I have.

What did you cook? And who ate it?

Language lab 2

GIVING A PRESENTATION

1 Read. What is Mark's presentation about? Check ☑.

Today I'm going to talk about going to the dentist! Have you ever cried because your mom said "It's time to go to the dentist"? I used to do that, but then I talked about it with my parents and I stopped feeling scared. First of all, dentists are very important in our lives because they take care of our teeth. Having healthy teeth is essential. Secondly, you should remember that if you brush your teeth regularly, your dentist won't have much to do. So, your visits to the dentist won't hurt. In conclusion, dentists have an important role and we need to work with them, not be afraid of them.

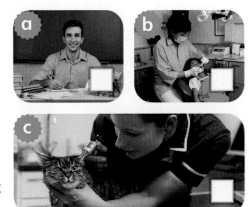

2 Read and put Mark's ideas in order. Underline the words and phrases in the text that help order Mark's ideas.

a   Mark doesn't worry about seeing the dentist anymore. ☐

b   You can help your dentist take care of your teeth. ☐

c   Most children don't like dentists. ☐

d   You mustn't be afraid of your dentist. ☐

e   We need dentists in our lives to have healthy teeth. ☐

I'm going to talk about …

Have you **ever** …?

First of all, …

Secondly, …

In conclusion, …

3 Prepare a short presentation about one of the topics below. Find some pictures or things that can make your presentation more interesting. Remember to organize your ideas.

Someone or something you are afraid of

A special place

A place you dream of visiting

The importance of eating healthy food

A sport you enjoy watching and/or playing

4 Give your presentation in small groups. Ask a question after each presentation.

8 My amazing city

1 ▶ **Watch. Order the questions based on the answers in the game.**

a Where would you go if you could go anywhere? ☐

b What would you do if you were a millionaire? ☐

c What would you change if you could change anything on Earth? ☐

2 ▶ **Read and complete with the correct form of the verbs in the box. Watch to check.**

be (2)   buy   give   go   protect

1 If I could change anything on Earth, I _____ the environment.

2 If I could go anywhere, I _____ to the Antarctic.

3 If I _____ a millionaire, I _____ a castle for my mom and dad.

4 If I _____ a millionaire, I _____ most of it to charity.

3 **What would you do if you were a millionaire? Write 4 chain sentences to see how your life would change. Follow the pattern.**

CODE CRACKER

If I were a millionaire, I would have a swimming pool in my yard. If I had a swimming pool in my yard, I would swim every day. If I swam every day, I would be very fit. If I were very fit, I would go to the Olympics.

_____

_____

_____

_____

Language lab 1

SECOND CONDITIONAL

I will learn the Second Conditional.

1 Read the message. How many requests does Claudia make? Check ☑.

three requests ☐   four requests ☐   five requests ☐

A message to our mayor

Dear Mayor,

My name's Claudia and I'm sending you this message because my neighborhood needs some changes. First of all, the trash cans are so old that they don't close. If they closed properly, cats wouldn't take the trash out and our roads would look cleaner. Another problem is that the sidewalks are full of holes. If someone walked in a hole, they could fall and break a leg or an arm. Also, the crosswalks are fading away. The paint is getting old and they're hard to see. This is dangerous and there could be accidents. Lastly, we would really like to have a park. If we had a park, we wouldn't play in the streets. I hope you'll listen to these requests and make the changes in the near future.

Thank you for your time.

Claudia Riggs

2 Read again. Check ☑ the correct sentences and rewrite the incorrect ones.

1   If the trash cans were new, monkeys wouldn't get to them.   ☐

_____

2   The rivers would be easier to see if they painted them again.   ☐

_____

3   If there was a park, the children wouldn't play in the streets.   ☐

_____

🇬🇧 British	🇺🇸 American
rubbish bins	trash cans
pedestrian crossing	crosswalk
pavement	sidewalk

If I were the mayor of this town	,	**I'd build** a stadium here.
There wouldn't be an overpass here		if **there wasn't** so much traffic.
Where **would** you **play**		if **there wasn't** a park in your town?

3 Read again. Underline the Second Conditional sentences.

35

4 Match to make sentences.

1 If there wasn't that office building in front of our house,
2 I'd live in an apartment in a skyscraper
3 I'd feel really scared
4 If there were more trees in the city,
5 My brother wouldn't have to leave town

a the air would be cleaner.
b we'd have a better view of the mountains.
c if there was a college here.
d if I had to walk through a tunnel in the dark.
e if I moved to a big city.

5 Complete the questions with the correct form of the verbs.

1 If you _____ (can) move to a big city, where would you go?

2 If you could choose someone to have a statue of in your town, who _____ _____ (it, be) ?

3 What would you change in your neighborhood if you _____ (be) your town's mayor?

4 If you _____ (have to) change something in your house/apartment, what would it be?

5 If the mayor told you to choose between a park and a pool, what _____ _____ (you, choose) and where _____ (you, place) it?

6 How would life on Earth change for people if there _____ (not be) any animals?

6 Ask and answer the questions in 5 with your partner. Discuss your ideas in pairs.

If you could move to a big city, where would you go?

If I moved to a big city, I think I'd go to Tokyo, Japan.

Really? Why?

I'm interested in Japanese culture and I love sushi! How about you? Where would you go?

Language lab 2

PREPOSITIONS OF MOVEMENT

I will ask for and give directions.

1 Read. Circle the correct prepositions.

So, that's the palace I was telling you about when we started our tour. I hope you enjoyed the tour. Now, for those who are hungry, there's a restaurant near here. Walk **1** _____ the square, to the other side over there, and you'll see it. If you walk **2** _____ this road and then enter the park **3** _____ the main park gate, you'll find a nice café there. Someone asked about the Science Museum. The fastest way is to walk **4** _____ the bridge and then **5** _____ the stadium. The museum will be on your left. Any more questions?

Tour guide

1	through	across	over
2	around	through	along
3	through	over	past
4	over	around	through
5	across	past	over

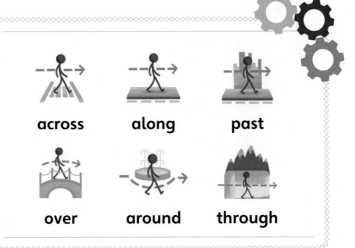

across   along   past

over   around   through

2 Read the question and look at the map. Write the answer.

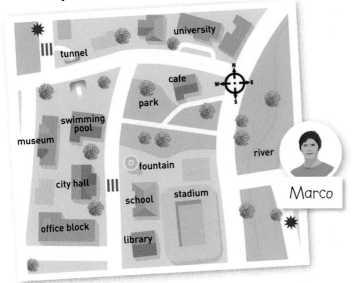

Marco

Marco: Sorry, what's the fastest way to the swimming pool?

_____

_____

3 Work in pairs. Ask and answer new questions with the map in 2.

Excuse me, can you tell me where the school is?

Sure! Walk along this road. Go past the swimming pool and the city hall. The school is across from the city hall.

Extra Grammar 1

PAST PERFECT

I will use the Past Perfect.

1 Read the text. Why is Louis Pasteur famous? Check ☑.

He is famous because he …

a   lived in Strasbourg. ☐   b   was a professor. ☐   c   fought diseases. ☐

Louis Pasteur was a French biologist and chemist. He was born in 1822. Before he became a university professor in Strasbourg, he had wanted to be a teacher.

Pasteur is famous for studying germs. He wanted to stop diseases like typhoid. After he had done many experiments, he discovered "germs" — bacteria that make people ill. Scientists hadn't studied these before. He also found a way to kill bacteria in milk to make the milk last longer. We still use his technique today; it's called pasteurization.

Pasteur also discovered that when he gave people a very weak form of a disease, they didn't get ill with the strong type. This is how he made vaccines that saved many people's lives. He gave the first rabies vaccine to a 9-year-old boy because a sick dog had bitten the boy. Today the Pasteur Institute in Paris continues Louis Pasteur's work against diseases.

2 Read again. Answer the questions with one word.

1   What had Louis wanted to be before he became a professor?

_____

2   What did he find that other scientists hadn't discovered before?

_____

3   What's the process called that makes milk last longer?

_____

4   What did Pasteur develop that saved many lives?

_____

> Before I became a scientist, I **had wanted** to become a musician.
>
> She **had studied** for many years before she became a doctor.
>
> **Had** they **studied** germs before?
>
> Yes, they **had**. / No, they **hadn't**.

3 Read again. Underline sentences in Past Perfect.

4 Match to make sentences.

1	I didn't have any money because	a	I had lost my keys.
2	She had never eaten sushi before	b	I had lost my wallet.
3	He didn't pass his exam because	c	he went there last year?
4	Had he been to London before	d	the party last week?
5	I couldn't get in the house after	e	he hadn't studied at all.
6	Had you ever met her before	f	she went to Japan.

5 Read the sentences and answer the question. Then circle to make the rules.

Part one

1 I had studied English for two years before

2 He had been a school teacher before

Part two

I went to live in London.

he stopped working.

a What happened earlier, Part one or Part two? _____

b We usually use Past Perfect with Simple Present / Simple Past .

c We use Past Perfect to talk about something that happened before / after something else.

6 Complete the story. Choose the correct verbs.

Let me tell you about how I 1 missed / had missed my train yesterday. After school I 2 went / had gone to a café with friends from my band. Our history teacher 3 gave / had given us a project to do, so we were talking about it. It 4 was / had been suddenly really late! I 5 ran / had run to the station really quickly, but when I got there, the train 6 left / had left ! It was my fault. I 7 didn't look / hadn't looked at the time because I was having too much fun.

7 Look at 6. Create your own story and include at least 3 sentences in Past Perfect. Then act out the story to your class.

Extra Grammar 2

VERBS + GERUND, VERBS + *TO*-INFINITIVE

1 Read the conversation. What homework does Nadia have to do this evening? Circle.

She has to study French / do math / write an essay .

Rosy: Are you ready? You promised to go swimming with me!

Nadia: I know and I really want to go, but our teacher gave us so much homework! I need to memorize this list of French words, do five math problems, and write an essay for tomorrow!

Rosy: Are you sure it's all for tomorrow?

Nadia: Of course! Look! Here's my notebook!

Rosy: I think you should try reading instructions more slowly. The math homework is for next week, and the French words are for Friday.

Nadia: Are you sure?

Rosy: Of course, here, look at your teacher's note.

Nadia: Wow, that's great! I love swimming! I'll get my things and we can go.

Rosy: What can we do afterwards? I suggest going for a smoothie at the café.

Nadia: Oh yes! Come on, let's go!

2 Read and match.

1	Nadia promised	a	she has a lot of homework.
2	Nadia really wants to go but she thinks	b	swimming.
3	Nadia should try	c	to go swimming with Rosy.
4	Nadia says she loves	d	reading instructions more slowly.

Verbs followed by a gerund

I **love speaking** French.

Do you **mind helping** me with dinner?

If I **keep practicing**, will I get better at tennis?

Verbs followed by *to* + verb

He **learned to swim** last week.

We **decided to do** the project together.

I **hope to travel** to China one day.

They **prefer to watch** a movie tonight.

3 Read the text on page 40 again. Underline the verbs followed by a gerund in blue and the verbs followed by a *to*-infinitive in green.

4 Complete the dialog with the correct form of the verbs.

> decide   keep   mind   need   promise   suggest   would love

Dad: Do you 1 _____ to finish your history essay this week?

Jenny: Yes! I finally chose a topic. I 2 _____ to write about the Romans.

Dad: That's interesting. Do you 3 _____ showing it to me when you finish it? I 4 _____ to read it.

Jenny: Sure! But can you help me find some information? You 5 _____ to help me, remember?

Dad: OK. I 6 _____ looking online, but we should also look at books. Don't trust everything you read on the internet.

Jenny: I know, I know. You 7 _____ saying that. Let's get started today.

5 Complete the sentences with the gerund or the to-infinitive form of the verbs in parentheses.

1 What do you enjoy _____ (do) when you don't have homework?

2 I keep _____ (forget) about my dad's birthday. I'll put it on my calendar.

3 How did you learn _____ (cook) so well? Who taught you?

4 We hope _____ (see) you soon. When can you come again?

6 Complete the sentences so they are true for you. Then walk around the class and find classmates who feel the same way.

1 This year, I've decided _____ .

2 I usually don't mind _____ .

3 Next year, I promise _____ .

Next year, I promise to help with housework more. What about you?

No, not me. I promise to practice speaking English more.

Extra Grammar 3

IF I WERE YOU … AND I WISH …

I will learn to use **If I were you** and **I wish**.

1 Read. Write the jobs Leon and his dad mention. Circle the job Leon wants to do in the future.

_____ .

Dad: What are you going to do when you leave school, Leon?

Leon: I'm good at math and I like kids. I like explaining things to other people, so I think I want to be a math teacher.

Dad: That's a good idea … but … if I were you, I'd become a soccer player.

Leon: But Dad, I'm not that good at soccer. I wish I was better at it!

Dad: OK … Well, you're intelligent and good at science. You could be a doctor.

Leon: No, Dad. I feel sick if I see blood. I wish I didn't …

Dad: You like books and law. You could be a lawyer.

Leon: I'd hate that! I don't like reading big boring books.

Dad: Yes … well, you're also brave and you love adventures. If I were you, I'd be a firefighter.

Leon: I wish I was brave, but I like math. I know it's hard to believe. Do you wish you were a soccer player, Dad?

Dad: Yes, I do!

2 Read again and write T (True), F (False), or DS (Doesn't Say).

1 Leon has a good idea about what he wants to do in the future. _____

2 Leon isn't good at soccer, but he's good at other sports. _____

3 Leon doesn't like seeing blood. _____

4 Leon likes reading books about law. _____

🇬🇧 British	🇺🇸 American
maths	math

3 Read again. Underline sentences with *If I were you* in green and circle sentences with *wish* in blue.

If I were you, I'd study to become a scientist.

I wouldn't become a doctor **if I were you.**

I wish I was better at soccer.

I wish I could run faster.

I wish I didn't have to get up early.

4 Put the words in order.

1 spoke / I / I / wish / well. / Spanish

_____

2 songs. / I / could / wish / write / I

_____

3 I / were / play / all day. / I / wouldn't / you, / If / video games

_____

4 I'd / I / a / you. / if / were / graphic designer / become

_____

5 wish / I / so / I / shy. / wasn't

_____

6 you, / If / study / were / I / law. / I'd

_____

5 Look at the photos. What do you think each person is wishing for? Write sentences with I wish.

1 _____

_____

2 _____

_____

3 _____

_____

4 _____

_____

6 Write advice for the children in the photos in 5. Use If I were you.

1 If I were you, _____ .

2 _____ .

3 _____ .

4 _____ .

Grammar Reference

Unit 1

Language lab 1

Reported speech – present to past (statements):

"I *ride* my bike to school."
He said that he *rode* his bike to school.

"I *take* the subway. I don't want to be late."
She said that she *took* the subway. She *didn't want* to be late.

"They *go* to school by car."
She said that they *went* to school by car.

Language lab 2

Reported speech (questions):

"*Do you like* walking to school?"
She asked them *if they liked* walking to school.

"*What time do you take* the subway?"
They asked her *what time she took* the subway.

"*What do you do* after school?"
I asked him *what he did* after school.

Unit 2

Language lab 1

Relative clauses – *which, who, where, when, whose, that*:

He's the reporter *who* interviews famous actors.
This is the article *that* he wrote.
This is *where* his online articles are uploaded.
That was the evening *when* he met the movie director.
He's the reporter *whose* article won a competition.
Here's the interview *which* I read last week. It's very funny!

Language lab 2

***Used to* in affirmative and negative statements and questions:**

I *used to* read his movie reviews every week. I *didn't use to* watch his vlog. He *didn't use to* interview actors. He *used to* take photos.
My parents *used to* buy a newspaper every day. They *didn't use to* read the news online.

Did people *use to* share news online?
No, they didn't.

Did she *use to* write a blog?
Yes, she did.

Unit 3

Language lab 1

Modals for obligations and advice (*have to/don't have to/must/mustn't/ should/shouldn't*):

You *should* stand in line outside the classroom.
You *shouldn't* talk when the teacher is talking.
You *mustn't* eat in the library.
They *must* take the test next week.
You *have to* walk in the hallway.
He *has to* go to the principal's office!
They *don't have to* go to assembly today.
She *doesn't have to* go to detention.

Language lab 2

Modals to ask for favors (*could/would*):

Would you help me study for the test, please?
Could you do me a favor and open the door, please?
Would you give this pen to Joe, please?
Could I share your book, please?

Unit 4

Language lab 1

Future using *will*, *going to*, or the Present Progressive:

We *will* go to Japan in the future.
It *won't* be too expensive.
I'm *going to* eat sushi.
My brother is *going to* love Tokyo!
I'm buying a guide book tomorrow.

Do you know where you *will* stay?
We *will* stay in a hotel.

Are you *going to* see any cherry blossoms?
Yes, I hope so.

Language lab 2

Might and will for future possibilities and certainties:

The weather **might** be sunny in Japan. It's spring.
We **might** hike up a mountain or visit a waterfall.
We **might not** go shopping every day, but I want to buy some souvenirs for my friends.

It **will** be busy in Tokyo. It's a big city.
We **will** visit a palace. It's in a beautiful park.
We **won't** speak Japanese.

Grammar Reference

Unit 5

Language lab 1

Past Passive:

The product *was invented* three years ago.
It *was designed* by a conservationist who wanted to protect the environment.
It *wasn't sold* in shops. It *was sold* online.
The profits *weren't spent* by the inventor.
They *were given* to charity.

Language lab 2

Past Passive questions:

Where *was* the product *invented*?
It *was invented* in Sweden.

When *was* the advertisement *made*?
It *was made* two years ago.

What *were* the shoes *made* from?
They *were made* from recycled materials.

Why *were* the shoes *wanted* by everyone?
Because they *were worn* by a famous basketball player.

Were the shoes *sold* in many countries?
Yes, they were.

Unit 6

Language lab 1

Present Perfect Progressive with *for* and *since*:

Have you *been waiting* here *for* long?
I've *been waiting* for you *since* ten o'clock!
She's *been studying* in the library *for* two hours.
He *hasn't been reading* for long.
What have they *been doing* *since* school finished?

Language lab 2

Present Perfect with *just*, *already*, *yet*, and *still*:

Have you chosen a book *yet*?
Yes, *I've **already** found* an interesting book. It's about endangered animals.

He ***still** hasn't finished* reading that book about ancient Rome. He needs more time.

We've ***just** seen* a movie about pyramids.

Unit 7

Language lab 1

Present Perfect and Simple Past:

Have you ever cooked lunch for your family?
Yes, I have.

When **did** you **cook** lunch?
I cooked lunch for my family last week.

Have you and your parents ever eaten vegan food?
Yes, we have!

What **did** you **eat**?
We ate vegan burgers. I often make them for my family.

Language lab 2

Presentation skills:
Tips on how to plan your presentation:

- Write brief notes to remind you of the key points.
- Use short, simple sentences.
- Speak clearly and loudly.
- Practice your presentation in front of other people if you can.
- Make eye contact with the people you're talking to.
- End the presentation with a conclusion or summary.

Unit 8

Language lab 1

Second Conditional:

If I were older, *I'd* travel to lots of countries.
If we had more money, *we'd* stay in expensive hotels.
He'd do a student exchange program *if he had* more time.
They wouldn't go camping *if they didn't have* a camper van.
If they lived nearer to the airport, *would they* go abroad more often?

Language lab 2

Prepositions of movement (*across*, *along*, *past*, *over*, *around*, *through*):

How do we get to the departure gate?
We've walked *around* the airport for ages!

First, go *over* the bridge to get to the other terminal.
Then you need to go *past* check-in.
You have to go *through* security.
Walk straight *across* the hall.
Then go *along* the hallway to the departure gate.

Pearson Education Limited
KAO TWO
KAO Park
Hockham Way
Harlow, Essex
CM17 9SR
England

and Associated Companies throughout the world.

english.com/englishcode

First published 2021

ISBN: 978-1-292-35456-9

Set in Heinemann Roman 12pt
Printed and bound by CPI Group (UK) Ltd, Croydon CR0 4YY

Image Credits:

123RF.com: Andrey Bzhitskikh 29, auremar 31, Cathy Yeulet 17, 33,
Iakov Kalinin 23, Jaren Wicklund 31, Noppadon Sakulsom 20; **Pearson
Education Ltd:** Jon Barlow 8, 9, 16,, 28, 32, 36, 37, 41, Jules Selmes 37,
Tudor Photography 33; **Photodisc:** Kim Steele 29; **Shutterstock.com:** 4,
1390159 27, Africa Studio 33, Anna Jedynak 29, Billion Photos 29, Christy
Thompson 43, Costas Anton Dumitrescu 24, CREATISTA 5, Dragon Images
16, ejwhite 40, Elena Elisseeva 19, Ermolaev Alexander 43, f11photo 36,
farres 22, Federico Rostagno 23, Flamingo Images 35, goir 3, 5, 7, 9, 11, 12,
15, 17, 18, 19, 20, 21, 25, 27, 29, 30, 31, 35, 37, hamdan 22, Image Wizard 38,
iofoto 17, Jim Barber 22, Kitch Bain 13, Kung Min Ju 5, Kzenon 8, Leonid
Andronov 25, LifeHD 9, Liv Oeian 11, Maya Kruchankova 15, Nick Fox 7,
nicostock 11, Oksana Mizina 43, Oleg Golovnev 38, PHB.cz (Richard Semik)
32, Photographee.eu 43, pixelheadphoto digitalskillet 42, Pj photography
13, Scott Rothstein 22, Therese Elaine 13, VaLiza 15, VGstockstudio 39,
Zurijeta 21

Video Screenshots: Jungle Creative

All other images © Pearson Education

Illustrated by Milli-Jane Pooley/Lemonade Illustration, p. 37 (right);
Martin Sanders/Beehive Illustration, p. 37.

Cover Image: *Front:* **Pearson Education Ltd:** Jon Barlow